A
MODERN
SHAMAN'S
GUIDE TO A
PREGNANT
UNIVERSE

A
MODERN
SHAMAN'S
GUIDE TO A
PREGNANT
UNIVERSE

by
Christopher S. Hyatt, Ph.D.
&
Antero Alli

NEW FALCON PUBLICATIONS
TEMPE, ARIZONA, U.S.A.

International Standard Book Number: 1-56184-241-9
Library of Congress Catalog Card Number: 88-81430

First Edition 1988
Second Edition 2006

Cover by Jason Beam

Those expecting a reply should enclose a stamped, self-addressed envelope. Foreign correspondents should enclose international reply coupons.

The paper used in this publication meets the minimum requirements of the American National Standard for Permanence of Paper for Printed Library Materials Z39.48-1984

Address all inquiries to:
NEW FALCON PUBLICATIONS
1739 East Broadway Road #1-277
Tempe, AZ 85282 U.S.A.

(or)
320 East Charleston Blvd. #204-286
Las Vegas, NV 89104 U.S.A.

website: http://www.newfalcon.com
email: info@newfalcon.com

This book is dedicated to:

Timothy Leary, Ph.D.
   Scientist
   Cyber-Punk
   Neuro-Hero
   Philosopher

CAUTION:

POSITIVE — — — — — — — NEGATIVE
MASCULINE — — — — — — FEMININE
RADIANT — — — — — — — MAGNETIC
DRY — — — — — — — MOIST
STRONG — — — — — — — WEAK
COLD — — — — — — HOT
IMPORTANT — — — — — — INSIGNIFICANT
DOMINANT — — — — — — — SUBMISSIVE
STABLE — — — — — — — VOLATILE
MECHANICAL — — — — — — — SPONTANEOUS
GOOD — — — — — — — EVIL
PLEASURE — — — — — — — PAIN
YOUNG — — — — — — — OLD
COMMITTED — — — — — — — INDIFFERENT
BEAUTIFUL — — — — — — — UGLY
REASON — — — — — — — INTUITION
HARD — — — — — — — SOFT
JOY — — — — — — — SORROW
CREATIVE — — — — — — — DESTRUCTIVE
ILLUSION — — — — — — — REALITY
CLEAR — — — — — — — DENSE
OPEN — — — — — — — CLOSED
SURPRISE — — — — — — — PLAN
FREEDOM — — — — — — — SLAVERY
CERTAIN — — — — — — — UNCERTAIN

When you are done performing this book please re-take the test and compare your answers. Remember we are using the word book lightly as it is really a vertical word pharmacy.

—Caution, handle gently, this is a newborn and you are its mid-wife.—

DANGER DANGER THIS WILL CHANGE YOUR BIO-CHEMISTRY

TABLE OF
PREGNANT PHASES

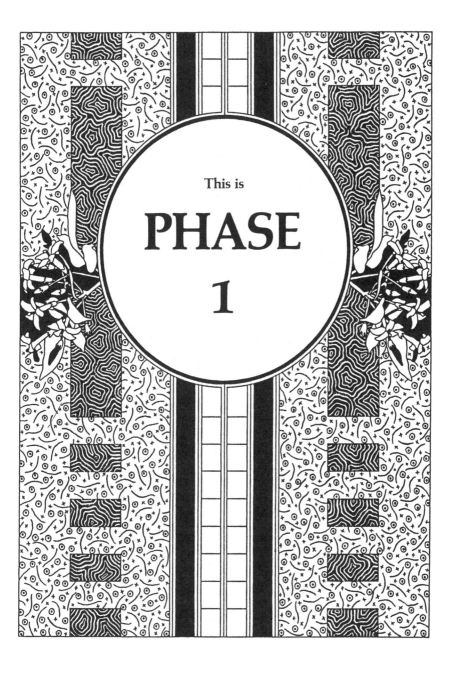

This is

PHASE

1

The Planet Earth Is In Labor

FACIT OMNIA LÆTA

AND

We Are the Mid-Wives

TO

A PREGNANT UNIVERSE

Why? Is The Planet Pregnant?

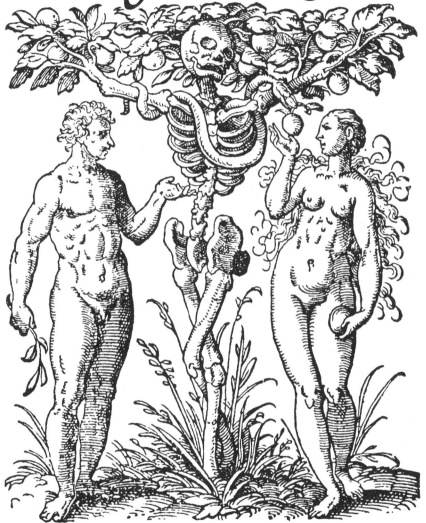

Because It is Suffering from a
Bad Conscience

Why?

(The Human Nervous Systems
inhabiting the Planet have
denied its instincts,
damaged its body and
ignored the powers
of its brain.
It has Betrayed Itself . . .
Or has It been Betrayed?)

Somehow all of this leads to a lurid yet
mysterious love affair. We are now left with
Its unborn child. What's a Mother to DO? As
mid-wives our imminent task is creating a
Neural-ecology . . . the feeding, caring, sheltering and provision of
opportunity for the nervous system.

NOTE: The Planet Has a Mate.

EMERGENCY ALERT:

The Planet has Mated
with its Inhabitants.
The ultimate
Interstellar Incestual Taboo,
forbidden for millennia.

BRACE
YOURSELF

Culture is NOTHING BUT the interactions between Genes and Geography.
This has been the secret of all planetary bar-tenders and global mixologists.
As we now know it is not the glass, but the cocktail that gets you high.
Culture, like words, is only ANY empty container.

A Modern Shaman's Guide to a Pregnant Universe

The Human Neural System is the most important and valuable instrument for

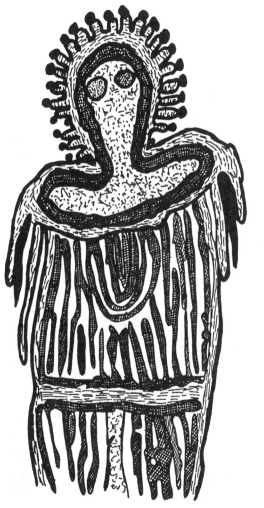

transmutation
and
personal
pleasure.

Planet Earth

has been selected to lead the way in repairing and preparing its futures

PREPARING!FOR!MILLENNIUM!MADNESS

We are drawing near Delivery Time, we the Mid-Wives, are WEAVING the nest for the coming Child.

And pray tell who is this Child, this Neural Messiah? Does She have a Name, a Face, a Number?

You May NOW Stand.

and _Who_ is _She ?_

(Description to Follow.)

She is Multiple rather than Singular

She is Many rather than One

She is Omni-Directional rather than Uni-Directional

She is Mobile rather than Gravitational

She is Time Free rather than Time Bound

She carries her possessions in a sack

She is Nomadic rather than Domestic

She gets High off her own Neurons

Her Territory is Everywhere

A Modern Shaman's Guide to a Pregnant Universe

Q. As a baby coming into this world does She need protection?

A. YES and NO.

As Her time approaches and the waves of contractions grow closer together, she feels the urge to reach out to the support of warm flesh.

She requires immediate contact . . . living committed

Neural Engagement.

We,
the Living, are
Her Mid-Wives,
and We the Living
are Her.
Remember,
"We the living
are a threat
to the Dead."

(Angel Tech:
Falcon, 1987).

If need be, are You willing to enter the Intensive Care Unit (The Eye-See-You) ?

☐ How are you preparing yourself for the Delivery Room, the Nursery?

☐ What Names are you considering for the Child?

☐ What is its Sign?

Its signs are all and none
(See the Pharmaceutical Astrology Section.)

WHAT'S NEW?

The new Birth is a Planet Full of Possibilities—High Load—Minimum Impedance . . .

The Baby Gods
can only incubate
inside
Omni-directional Consciousness.

Her greatest threat is a Womb without a View.

An unvented Womb, Knotted with Restriction

Planet Birth is Our Choice.

Her first sound is our Motto:

"Get High On Your Own Supply."

What is the Supply?

"The Neural Crapshoot"

PROPOSITION ONE: Words are empty vessels.
(Which vessels are you spilling yourself into?)

**PROPOSITION TWO:
The process of spilling is automatic.**
(Which vessel would you prefer spilling into?)

PROPOSITION THREE: How you live and breathe is a function of knowing how to spill and how to contain. Also known as personal styles of spilling and containing.

The passion energy poured into empty word vessels determines the power and quality of the inter-dimensional collision known as (pro and re) creation.

"All the realities we shall ever know are created by the conversation between DNA and CNS (Central Nervous System).

"The DNA Blueprint of evolution, past and future, can be deciphered as we tap into the DNA-CNS channel (dialogue)."

— Dr. Tim, from *The Intelligence Agents*,
Falcon Press, 1988

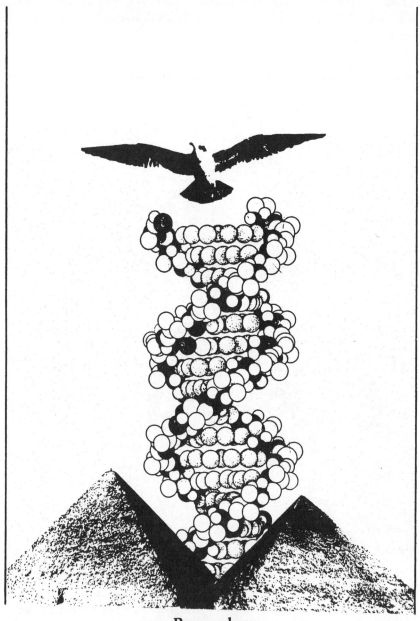

Re-member:
Artifacts (all Art & Facts) are the result of the dialogue of the developing DNA-CNS transaction and the medium (geography) womb nest feeding its growth.

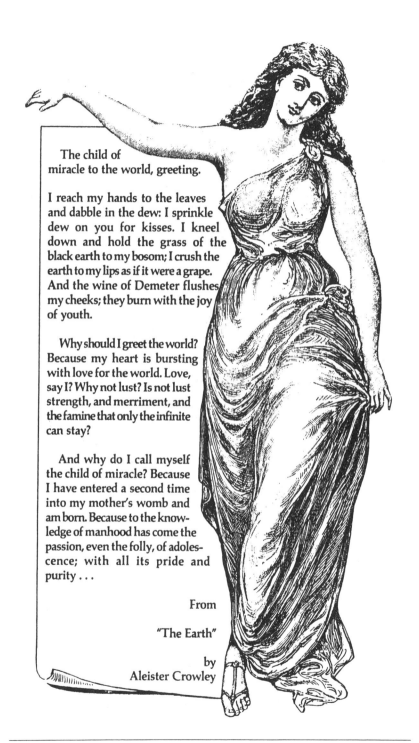

The child of
miracle to the world, greeting.

I reach my hands to the leaves
and dabble in the dew: I sprinkle
dew on you for kisses. I kneel
down and hold the grass of the
black earth to my bosom; I crush the
earth to my lips as if it were a grape.
And the wine of Demeter flushes
my cheeks; they burn with the joy
of youth.

Why should I greet the world?
Because my heart is bursting
with love for the world. Love,
say I? Why not lust? Is not lust
strength, and merriment, and
the famine that only the infinite
can stay?

And why do I call myself
the child of miracle? Because
I have entered a second time
into my mother's womb and
am born. Because to the knowledge of manhood has come the
passion, even the folly, of adoles-
cence; with all its pride and
purity . . .

From

"The Earth"

by
Aleister Crowley

This is

PHASE
2

A Baby is Born!!

a MODERN Shaman is a Shaman in the 21st Century

From the Greek, CYBER is a pilot

A Modern Shaman is an individual of power interacting with "spirits," for triggering Knowledge, Vision, Technology and Advanced Fun.

What, pray tell, are "spirits"?

(We're so glad you asked.)

SPIRITS are inside anything alive. EVERYTHING IS ALIVE. There's just one catch, though.

You have to know you're alive to know this. How do you know you're
ALIVE ? !

A Modern Shaman's Guide to a Pregnant Universe

How can we know anything at all?

6   LOVERS

The DNA/CNS transactions.

If we exchange "neural" for SPIRITS & DEMONS, the CYBER-SHAMAN is piloting Hir neurology (CNS) and, is a functional Neural Engineer.

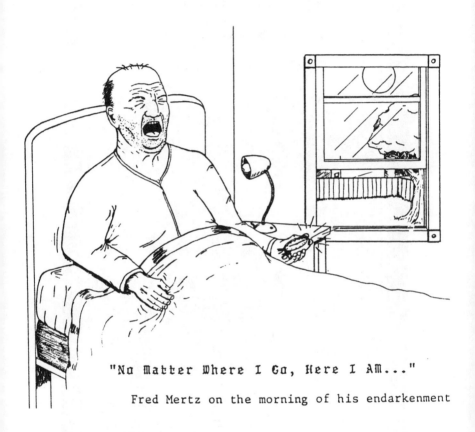

"No matter where I Go, Here I AM..."

Fred Mertz on the morning of his endarkenment

NOTE: Not all engineers are boring, sterile, bland personalities.

A Modern Shaman's Guide to a Pregnant Universe

Yet all suffer (occasionally) from the same dismal malady.
This has nothing to do with
INTENTIONAL SUFFERING FOR FUTURE FUN.
(That will be introduced later on.)

SURPRISE!
is DNA's way of letting CNS know It's always there.

Real Surprise
activates a
neuro-chemical panacea for

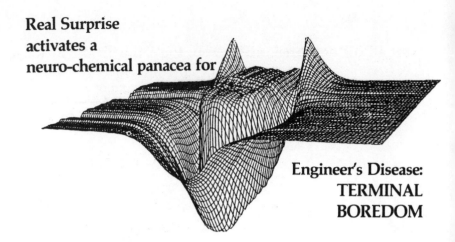

Engineer's Disease:
TERMINAL
BOREDOM

A Modern Shaman knows how and when to administer the intermittent shocks of SURPRISE . . . to Hirself & Others for minimizing the symptoms of Engineer's Disease.

This cyber technique will be referred to hereafter as:

ALTERING
THE
EXPECTED

and is the primary catalyst for creating the hedonic drugs of
IMPROVISATIONAL TURNONS.

Another cyber function of the BRAIN decodes current information into skills for navigating the future & accessing
Future Memory

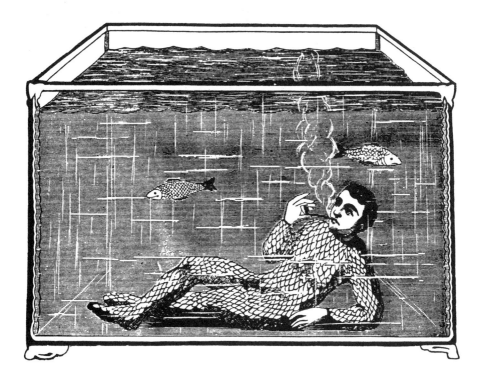

(IT PAYS TO BE ALERT WHEN THERE'S NEW DRUGS IN TOWN)

As a modern shaman responds to the continuing flux and interplay between her DNA/CNS, environment and technology...

SHe learns how to gain access

to Hir very own

PHARMACY . . .

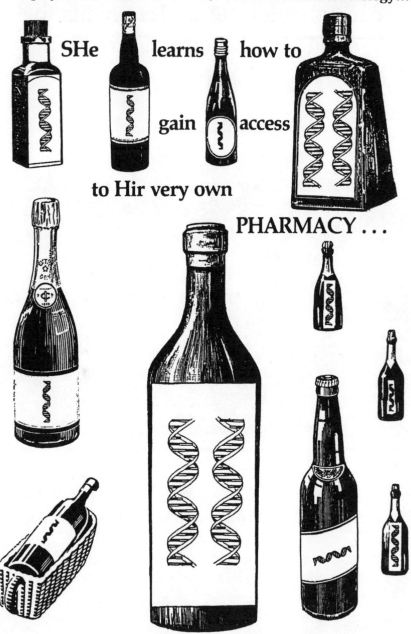

A Modern Shaman's Guide to a Pregnant Universe

Piloting your own path does not mean that you are just selfish and oblivious to what others are doing. Any good pilot checks in with other pilots, asking questions like:

Where are you
How's the weather out there
Which way is the wind blowing
How are the swells **?**

The Cyber Shaman needs to be attentive to
other people because
SHe knows SHe's on Hir own.

THOUGHTS ARE DRUGS.
Sobriety is Being Here, Zen.

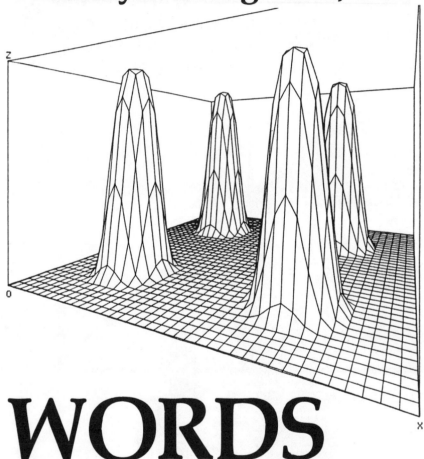

WORDS
are trance-induction drugs.

The Cyber-Shaman engages and disengages Word Trance as a way to invoke the spirits necessary for Hir Work.

Just How Does Word Trance Work?

Any thought or image tends to create a similar and sometimes identical neural-psychological reaction as the "real outer event" it is referring to.

(For the sake of clarity alone, "real" simply means an "out there event" as an "in-there event" reflects a "DNA-CNS-MIND event.")

Sometimes an image of a car hitting you can create a similar neural-physiological reaction to the "real" event of a car actually hitting neuro-muscular-bone you.

A Modern Shaman's Guide to a Pregnant Universe

Sometimes, people kill themselves by creating in-there emergency events. Historically, this has been called:

VOODOO DEATH.

This notion demonstrates the potency of our psycho-neural-biology interactions.

How much longer will you keep creating
"unconscious" (automatic) Inside Emergency States
which seek Outside Confirmation to affirm

HOW
CREATIVE
YOU
REALLY
ARE ? ! ? !

A Modern Shaman's Guide to a Pregnant Universe

the PRIMARY STRATEGY of the CYBER-SHAMAN

To respond to the internal potency of CREATION. To create Inside Emergency States that are FUN and INSTRUCTIVE which, in turn, seek Outside Confirmation to affirm.

HOW
CREATIVE

YOU
CAN
BE

THE
CYBER—SHAMAN
LIVES

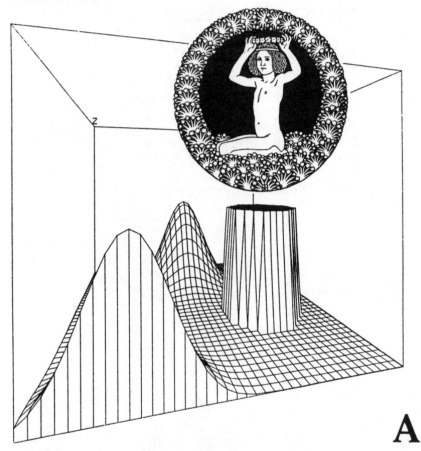

A
VOODOO LIFE.

A Modern Shaman's Guide to a Pregnant Universe

This is

PHASE
2.3

WORDS TRIGGER AUTONOMIC — —
RE-ACTIVITY — — — —
CREATING YOUR OWN NEURO — — —
PHARMACY

THE FOLLOWING SECRET OF STATE-DEPENDENT KNOWLEDGE HAS BEEN HIDDEN FROM MANKIND FROM THE FALL TO THE RISE OF PLANETARY INCEST.
(Refer to Beginning Story)

CONSCIOUSNESS IS NOT JUST A WORD. IT COMES IN # # # DEGREES # # # WHICH CAN BE MEASURED LIKE HEAT AND COLD. WHAT FOLLOWS PROVIDES YOU WITH A MANUAL OF INTER-GALACTIC KNOWLEDGE AND ACCESS.
IT WILL CHANGE YOUR OPERATING PROCEDURES.

— PROCEED WITH CAUTION —

A MODERN SHAMAN
Studies in EndocroKnowledgy

Most of what is learned, and imprinted and available for access is highly dependent on one's neuro-chemical-psycho-physiological state prior to, during and after the experience.

Simply we can liken this to a thermometer. Each degree of heat is associated with degree of consciousness. When a person is heated up, say on alcohol, the information learned and transmitted in this state is "associated" and dependent on the particular type of consciousness. From this knowledge we can begin to understand why certain information and knowledge is unavailable to us during certain degrees of excitement or depression.

One limitation that humans suffer from is the habit of not being able to create certain degrees of consciousness at will, thus being able to access and learn different types of information.

As important are the random changes of consciousness during the day. With each degree of consciousness, information is received and stored but is limited for retrieval due to the fact that particular degrees of consciousness can not be re-created as desired.

P.S. Degrees of Consciousness also limit AND provide access to different Brain Modules.

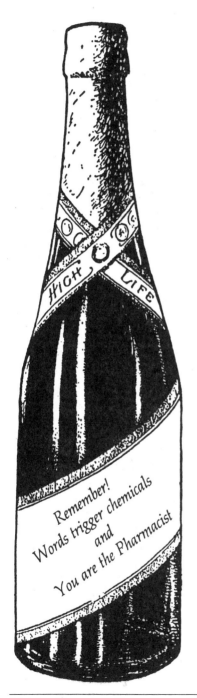

A goal
of a
modern
shaman
is to learn
to generate
degrees of
consciousness
at will. This
enables her to
learn, combine,
recombine and access
multiple levels of infor-
mation . . . information
infor . . . mation . . . information information . . . information . . . information
information . . . information . . . information . . . infor mation in for mation
information . . . information . . . information . . . information . . . information
informationinformationin
formationinformationin
formationinformation

Some of the methods and drug induction devices for learning how to "degree consciousness" are:

Improvisational Consciousness
(See *Pharmaceutical Astrology in this Book*)

Dream Consciousness
(See *Angel Tech*
and
The Dream Illuminati)

Hypnotic Trances
(See *Monsters & Magical Sticks*
and
Energized Hypnosis)

Exercise: Highs and Lows
(See *Undoing Yourself With Energized Meditation*
and
Radical Undoing)

Loaded Words
Self-Pharmacy Highs and Lows
(See *Undoing Yourself With Energized Meditation*
and
To Lie Is Human)

Imagination
(See *Monsters & Magical Sticks*
and
Energized Hypnosis)

Sexual Consciousness
(See *Sex, Drugs & Magick;*
Enochian World of Aleister Crowley;
Sex Magic, Tantra & Tarot;
and
Secrets of Western Tantra)

External Drugs
(See *Sex, Drugs & Magick*)

Games
(See *Monsters & Magical Sticks*
and
The Psychopath's Bible)

Events
(See *Undoing Yourself With Energized Meditation*)

Foods
(See *A Kabbalistic Cookbook*)

Ancient Ritual Knowledge
(See *The Golden Dawn Audio Series*)

Mind-Brain Exercises
(See *Undoing Yourself With Energized Meditation;*
Radical Undoing;
Prometheus Rising;
Quantum Psychology
and
Angel Tech)

(Perhaps you've noticed the predominance of Falcon's titles. Clever.)

Relaxation
(See *Energized Hypnosis)*

Yoga-type Exercises
(See *Radical Undoing)*

Meditations
(See *The You Meditation*
and
Zen Without Zen Masters)

Chaos
(See *Condensed Chaos;*
Prime Chaos;
PsyberMagick;
Shaping Formless Fire;
Seizing Power;
Taking Power;
The Pseudonomicon;
Beyond Duality;
Internal Texts
and
The Chaos Magic Audio Series)

Boredom
(Falcon publishes no boring books...except???)

Creating Emotions by Words and Images:
The Thought Pharmacy
(See *Monsters & Magical Sticks*
and
Energized Hypnosis)

Fights, Arguments
(See *What You Should Know About the Golden Dawn*)

Cyber-Books
(See *Info-Psychology;*
Neuropolitique
and
What Does WoMan Want?)

Alone and Together
(See *What Does WoMan Want?*)

Creating
(See *Sex, Drugs & Magick;*
Angel Tech;
and
Wilhelm Reich in Hell

Body
(See *Undoing Yourself With Energized Meditation*)

Kundalini
(See *Radical Undoing*)

Ceremonial Philosophies
(See *The Complete Golden Dawn System of Magic*
and
Ceremonial Magic & the Power of Evocation)

Magick
(See *The Eye in the Triangle;*
Enochian World of Aleister Crowley;
Ceremonial Magic and the Power of Evocation;
Kabbalistic Handbook for the Practicing Magician;
Kabbalistic Cycles and the Mastery of Life
and
The Golden Dawn Audio CDs)

Sexual Yoga
(See *Radical Undoing)*

Some Planetary Philosophies
(See *Buddhism & Jungian Psychology;*
The Psychopath's Bible;
The Black Books
and
To Lie Is Human)

Earth and Elsewhere
(See *Info-Psychology*
and
Neuropolitique)

Learning how "to degree" consciousness allows you to
modulate your neural-endocroKnowledgeable pharmacy,
creating drugs according to your needs and desires

Therefore
ALL FALCON BOOKS contain Endo cro Know ledgy

A Modern Shaman's Guide to a Pregnant Universe

CHANGE
Your Endocronology &

YOU
CHANGE

YOUR
FUTURES

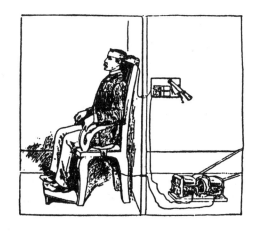

words that can kill (**LOCAL METAPHORS**) words that can kill

... words like **Mother, God, Country, Disco, Sex, Lawyer, Christmas, Hard Rock, Drugs, UFO, New Age, Commies, CIA, Channeling, Crystals** .

... and any other word with culturally pre-determined responses to:

Localized Shamans, or non-Shamans.

WORDS:

From the Cradle to the Grave.

FINIS CORONAT

A Modern Shaman's Guide to a Pregnant Universe

Metaphors operate as placebos,
creating and limiting
PAIN & PLEASURES.
Metaphor-Opiates & Hyper-Stimulants range from
God names to words for Food.
Certain phrases, or word combos, are ultra-sensitive and
contain enough depth and breadth to create predictable
emotive reactions . . .

(ranging from)

DEEP
PLEASURES

to

FURIOUS
RAGE

PLACEBOFORS
"Improvisational Turn Ons"

Placebofors trigger "readiness signals," preparing an automated responder (you and I) for action.

The inner landscape labors to organize *unfamiliar data* into "metaforms," triggering neuro-chemicals (brain-change of inner drug highs & lows) to activate our psycho-physical performances.

The ability to digest NEW placebofors feeds the brain NEW excitements, as well as a REST from eating LEFTOVERS (which certain brain parts persist in repeating).

Circumventing (short-circuiting) these older, worn-out chemical reactions is a sign of a direct hit for the CYBER-SHAMAN

Old . . .
Worn-Out
Drugs

Old placebofors can free-fall into a steady state of exhaustion, when a particular brain-part insists on re-hashing the same old problem in the same old way.

Nothing is Lost
through repetitions
except TIME

Conversations between the brain sectors which initiate communication are especially valuable.
By using different placebofors, new neuro-chemical buffers and short-circuits allow for immediate re-programming.

Get ready to fire up . . . . . .

Stubbornness to surrender a Metaform signifies that some part is unaware or unwilling to believe that new programs are more satisfying and revealing.

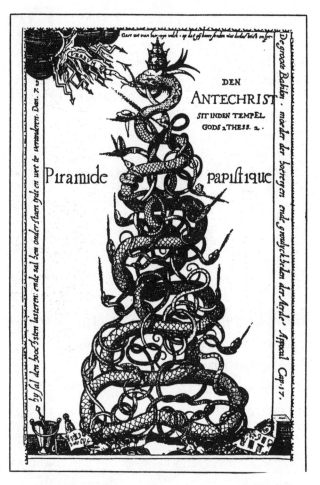

Identity shifts, losses gained, are temporary, like a roller coaster ride. Anxiety signals that old forms are preparing to believe you.

A Modern Shaman's Guide to a Pregnant Universe

The dynamics here are: that while you can rest assured to trust your sensitive brain, it sometimes finds you unaccepting of its messages. Let it know your willingness to be friends by feeding it something new and delectable.

MAKE
YOUR CHOICE
NOW

High wire acts of person brain-chemistry requires that you use something which is familiar, such as your ability to create images and emotions. Fill a word with a new emotion and image.

According to Dr. Heller, author of *Monsters and Magical Sticks* (Falcon Press, 1987),

> . . . Most systems experts contend that the way an individual speaks (conscious output), eye movements (unconscious input), and so-called "body language" add up to all of the individual's communication systems. I believe that there exists one more system: This system at first sounds complicated. As you become comfortable with it, you will discover that not only is it easy to understand, it may also be the key to a successful therapeutic outcome . . .

There's No Such Thing As HYPNOSIS?

There are many individuals, however, who claim that they are not making pictures, or who will claim that "I can't visualize." In reality, that cannot be true. In their personal reality, it is true for them. What that person is really saying is: "I am unable to become consciously aware of the images my mind is producing at this moment in time." In point of fact, they are generating pictures, or that person would not know what a chair is, or where they parked their car, but s/he is blocked as to conscious awareness of their internal pictures. Therefore, their visual system is, in this example, an:

Out of Conscious Unconscious System.

Dr. Heller is saying that "out of conscious systems" make it difficult for individuals
to "see, feel, sense or hear"
that there are choices
to be made
from
their
menu.

MENU

Our brain, a most delightful set of characters, knows exactly how to imitate something which holds a new future or excitement for it. The brain likes compliments.

The modern urban Shaman strikes a chord when he realizes that the brain is trying to convey a message which is hidden from his screen and personal developing lab. In otherwords he may deliberately freak out, take a rest, assume a God form. Doing something strange is the most normal reaction to being stuck out of consciousness.

JESUS CHRIST
IS OUR
LEADER

FOR THOSE WHO remember the last time they filled a pot with water, or those who recall how an unpleasant experience creates unpleasant feelings, let them dwell, idle for a moment on how they FILL words with neural-chemical meanings.

Words are beakers in your developing laboratory. Try an experiment. Fill one large container with water and try to make it fit into a smaller one. Let the residue pour over the counter onto the floor. Wiping it up requires some work, but the results can prevent you from slipping. Words overflow in the same way creating a mess or an opportunity to try out something new. Specify something you wish to clean up. Put it in an envelope and mail it to yourself. Open it when it arrives, reading it like a message from a friendly stranger. Using this model, you can help your brain develop you in a similar way. Send it a message, stamp it, mail it, and wait for a message. Are you aware what delivery system it chooses for you?

Send your brain a letter at least once a week.

TO: My Brain

Of transitory and sometimes of more interest than a person intends, are the side effects.

A shock to the nervous system often comes when we overdose ourself with familiarity

(Like a rat running from box to box.
Try taking a different path. Notice what is around you.)

During periods of restlessness, or when you just have a headache, simply take a different path to a familiar place. More often than not you will be surprised, a cure for most ailments, something not as incompatible as you might have guessed.

The less self-protective the ego is,

the more data

the brain
is willing to give it.

★ *FLASH* ★ *FLASH* ★ *FLASH* ★ *FLASH* ★ *FLASH* ★ *FLASH* ★ *FLASH* ★ *FLASH* ★

The brain can act as a pressor agent sending signals faster than the projectionist can flash them on the screen. When this occurs new routes can be chosen, to lessen the ego's sensitivity.

★ *FLASH* ★ *FLASH* ★ *FLASH* ★ *FLASH* ★ *FLASH* ★ *FLASH* ★ *FLASH* ★ *FLASH* ★

Temporary relief of data overdose can be as simple as a walk around the block or a bout of deep breathing. Don't use an antidote, instead send a signal back, that you appreciate the effort, but that you're not ready. Say No Thank You. Be polite when dealing with your brain. Tell it that you will send it a signal when you feel ready for more. Set up a time and place for a new meeting. *

[*Remember, your brain and you are not incompatible.]

NINO
"Nothing In, Nothing Out"

When you are familiar with your own dose, you can begin to speed up the process. Give your brain a gift, take it somewhere it hasn't been before. Do something "out of character." Your brain thirsts for diversity.

Normal consciousness (an oxymoron).

Life is a coma when you are.

NOTHING IN NOTHING OUT (NINO).

A Modern Shaman's Guide to a Pregnant Universe

Cure For Terminal
NINO

Terminal
NINO

Observe the brain for twitching or other signs of life. Feed information in small doses increasing its rate and depth of respiration. Be alert for a seizure. A good brain massage is in order. Clear yourself a path to a hot disco and dance. With adequate *circulation* and ventilation it will begin to rejuvenate itself.

THIS IS

PHASE

3

PHARMACEUTICAL-ASTROLOGY

Twelve Degrees of Consciousness Research

The CYBER-SHAMAN only has time to BE EVERYTHING. SHe moves with Hir totality if SHe moves at all. We are multi-trackers . . . selecting the course most effective to convey the intention at hand. Every day, a new ritual . . . every place, a different ceremony . . . certain rites for certain sites, in otherwords.

The only useful maps are those charting multi-directional currents, styles and territories. Anything less is one giant step backwards in to the realm of Infinite Regress.

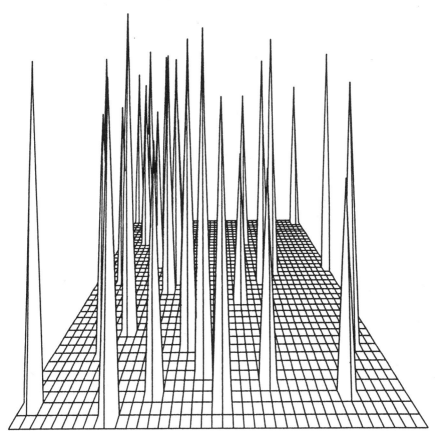

55. Random points with random heights. Most of the points were set to zero by the computer, which then chose points randomly to set to random values.

The NEW ASTROLOGY is not solar-emphasized.

It does not care what your sun sign is. Like the future of all governing systems, it is de-centralized and redistributes the power to each and every corner of your Central Nervous System.

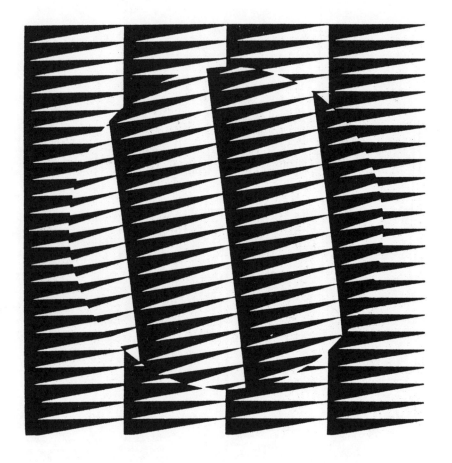

NOTE: NO CENTER REQUIRES YOUR FREEDOM. YOU ARE FREE TO ASK QUESTIONS. THERE ARE NO ANSWERS NECESSARY TO PROCEED.

Each of the 12 signs of the Zodiac, from ARIES to PISCES, are distinct styles in your Being which express multiplicity. These 12 Astro-Styles hang dormant as the various cloaks, hats and suits in the closet of your CNS-BRAIN Modules.

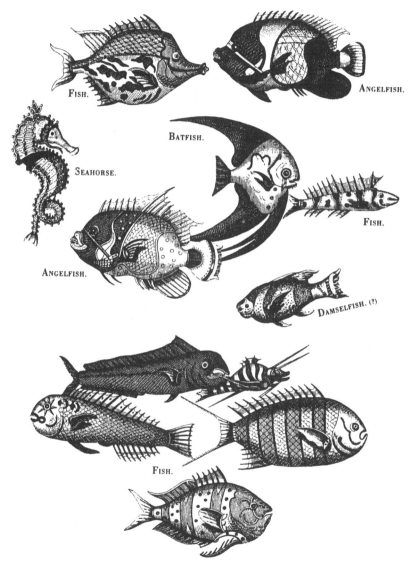

FISH.

ANGELFISH.

BATFISH.

SEAHORSE.

FISH.

ANGELFISH.

DAMSELFISH. (?)

FISH.

All twelve styles mark DEGREES OF CONSCIOUSNESS.

ALERT YOURSELF: STYLES are NOT answers. ANSWERS are ANTI-IMPROVISATIONAL SEDATIVES that will eventually put you to SLEEP.

An "Answer"

WARNING!
ANSWERS carry High Overdose Potential. ANSWERS are the Thrill That Kills. JUST SAY NO THANK YOU to Answers.

STYLE is only required when you're ON.

When your rehearsal period is over, you may proceed down the corridor to the next STAGE . . . the one marked "SHOWTIME." Until then, it's time to Clean Up Your Act by:

ASKING MORE QUESTIONS.

The following twelve Styles convey access points to various colors and facets of your MULTIDIMENSIONAL SELF. The neural engagement of your personal resonance determines the depth of access.

The following TWELVE DEGREES OF CONSCIOUSNESS are presented with the expressed intention of ushering you into your PHARMACY. Each DEGREE is a different drug. Through the activation of each style, TWELVE DRUGS are made available for your immediate neural engagement, pleasure and information.

Remember: INFORMATION IS NOW THE UNPREDICTABILITY OF A MESSAGE. The more unpredictable the message, the more INFORMATION there is in it.

TWELVE DEGREES OF CONSCIOUSNESS
Entry Commands, Buzzwords & Attributes

ARIES: The Source of FIRE. Impulse Power. No Holds Barred. As Blunt As Birth. In Charge to Discharge. Trusting the Thrust of Direct Transmission. Self-motivating. (adrenaline)

TAURUS: The Concentration of EARTH. Internal Security. Sitting Pretty. Stabilizing Influence. Sensual Grip. The Values of Propriety. Self-establishing Physicality. (tonic)

GEMINI: The Circulation of AIR. External Mobility. Conceptual Interaction. Distribution of Ideas. Decoding Perception. Maximum Flux. Self-diversifying. (stimulant)

CANCER: The Source of WATER. Emotional Force. Territorial Imperatives. Political Tactics. Clanning Instincts. The Law of Necessity. Felt Sense. Self-containing. (alcohol-based)

LEO: The Concentration of FIRE. Internal Drive/Dynamic Expression. High Style/Creative Performance. Personal Power and Innocent Pleasure. Self-radiating. (hedonic)

VIRGO: The Circulation of EARTH. Technical Knowledge. Discriminatory Power. Skillful Handling. Meticulous Preparation. Purity of Essence. Self-observing. (tonic-stimulant)

LIBRA: The Source of AIR. Social Perception. Protocol, Courtship and Intimacy. One-on-One Contacts. Diplomacy. Mutual Planning Between Partners. Self-offering. (hedonic-stimulant)

SCORPIO: The Concentration of WATER. Passionate Focus. Persistant, Enduring and Resourceful. Strategic Command. Powers to Transform. Self-fusion via surrender. (hallucinogenic-tonic)

SAGITTARIUS: The Circulation of FIRE. Perceptual Freedom. Expansion of Perspective. Supersensual/Intuitive Approach. Adventurous and Outgoing. Philosophical. Self-expanding. (hallucinogenic-stimulant)

CAPRICORN: The Source of EARTH. Attainment-oriented. Clarifying Professional Status. Fulfilling Executive Capacity. Administering Influence. Organized. Self-responsible. (tonic-hedonic-stimulant)

AQUARIUS: The Concentration of AIR. Autonomous Agent. Detachment Assuring Freedom to Interact. Idiosyncratic Approach. Unpredictable and Intermittent. Self-inventing. (hedonic-stimulant-hallucinogen)

PISCES: The Circulation of WATER. All-absorbing. Merging Into Everything. Impressionable Openness. Dissolution of Differences. Unifying Force. Self-sacrificing. (alcohol-based hallucinogen)

The previous TWELVE DEGREES OF CONSCIOUSNESS
are now available
for your IMMEDIATE ENGAGEMENT.

Each style potentially coincides and/or collides with the territory you're currently stalking . . . the experience you are HERE AND NOW passing through. As you express each Style, its DEGREE OF CONSCIOUSNESS can be drawn upon AT WILL to help synchronize your intention with whatever scene you're in.

AND/OR

With practice, each Style (DEGREE) develops enough force to determine an intention of its own thus, effecting change in the Out-There world.

This is how Synchronicity becomes a skill and Magick a reality.

Until then, however, experiment with one Style every day for the next twelve days. Like all effective, experimental LAB ACTIVITY, this only works if you DO IT EVERY DAY.

Long Term Objective: DO IT EVERY DAY until all twelve styles of your totality hold EQUAL VALUE for you. This will free you from Archetypal Chauvinism . . . Or, playing Astrological Favorites, so you may access more DEGREES OF CONSCIOUSNESS and hence . . . grow more conscious.

Fulfilling the Long-Term Objective will enable you to throw away the map and the key and . . . head straight into the

ACTION

If you really have to know anything after this point, NEW INFO will arrive daily, fresh from the NO COINCIDENCES DEPT., where Synchronicity is the STANDARD TIME ZONE.

PHASE 4
GOD
FORMS

Nietzsche said:

"For the individual to set up his own ideal and derive from it his laws, his pleasures, and his rights, that has perhaps been hitherto regarded as the most monstrous of all human aberrations, and as idolatry in itself; in fact, the few who have ventured to do this have always needed to apologize. It was marvelous art and capacity for creating Gods, in polytheism, that this impulse was permitted to discharge itself, it was here that it became purified, perfected, and ennobled.

"Monotheism, on the contrary, the rigid consequence of the doctrine of one normal human being, consequently the belief in a normal God, beside who there are only false, spurious Gods, has perhaps been the greatest danger of mankind in the past. In polytheism man's free-thinking and many-sided thinking has a prototype set up: the power to create for himself new and individual eyes, always newer and more individualized."

Of course
Nietzsche
was
mad
At _____ ?

Beware of  Mono-theism

BY   DR. TIM

Monotheism is the primitive religion which centers human consciousness on Hive Authority. There is One God and His Name is ————— (substitute Hive-Label).

If there is only One God then there is no choice, no option, no selection of reality. There is only Submission or Heresy. The word *Islam* means "submission." The basic posture of Christianity is kneeling. Thy will be done.

Monotheism therefore does no harm to hive-oriented terrestrials (Stages 10, 11 and 12) who eagerly seek to lay-off responsibility on some Big Boss.

Monotheism does profound mischief to those who are evolving to post-hive stages of reality. Advanced mutants (Stages 13 to 18) do make the discovery that "All is One," as the realization dawns that "My Brain creates all the realities that I experience."

The discovery of Self is frightening because the novitiate possessor of the Automobile Body and the Automobile Brain must accept all the power that the hive religions attributed to the jealous Jehovah.

The First Commandment of all monotheisms is: I am the Lord, thy God: Thou shalt have no other Gods before me. All monotheisms are vengeful, aggressive, expansionist, intolerant.

Stage 10: Islam-Catholicism
Stage 11: Protestant Evangelism
Stage 12: Communist-Dulles Imperialism.

It is the duty of a monotheist to destroy any competitive heresy. Concepts such as devil, hell, guilt, eternal damnation, sin, evil are fabrications by the hive to insure loyalty to Hive Central. All these doctrines are precisely designed to intimidate and crush Individualism.

The process of mutating into Self-hood plunges the mutant into his cross fire of neurogenetic moral flak. Most of the freak-outs, bad trips and hellish experiences are caused by Monotheistic Morality. Again, it must be emphasized, that Monotheism is a necessary stage. Monotheism is a technology, a tool, to bring pre-civilized tribespeople and caste-segregated primitives into the collectives necessary to develop the post-hive, post-terrestrial technologies.

The major evolutionary step is taken when the individual says: "There is only one God who creates the universe. This God is my Brain. As the driver of this Brain I have created a universe in which there are innumerable other Gods of equal post-hive autonomy—with whom I seek to interest. And my universe was, itself, created by a Higher Level of Divinity—DNA, whose mysteries and wonders I seek to understand and harmonize with."

— *Intelligence Agents*: Falcon Press, 1988

A Modern Shaman's Guide to a Pregnant Universe   89

Taking on God Forms

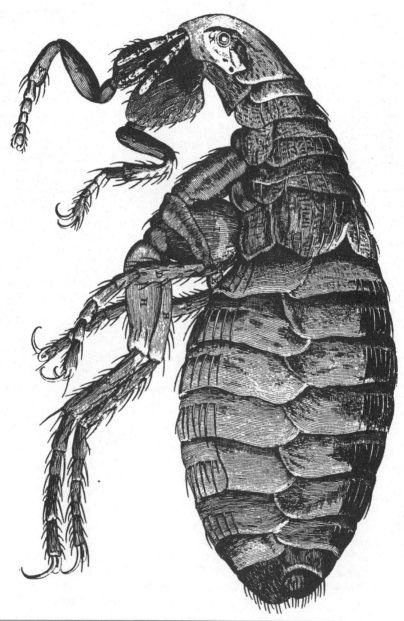

A Modern Shaman's Guide to a Pregnant Universe

One of the funniest, cutest and most entertaining of human habits is their automatic imitation of GODS. This has come to be known as the Most Dangerous Human Activity because humans cannot, for the life of them, remember the GODS they are imitating.

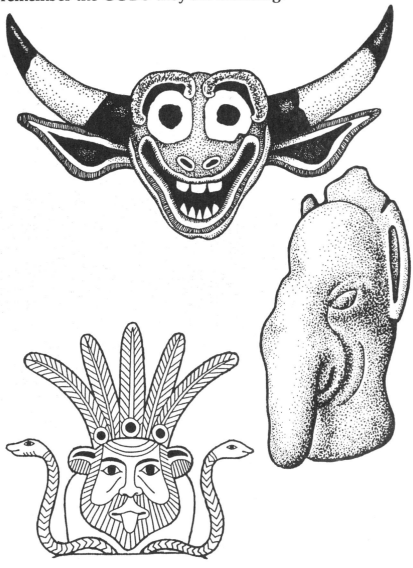

It has also been known to be EXCITING & CREATIVE to imitate GODS on purpose, switching up and back on the DEITY SCALE for GREATER FUN with HUMAN PROPHETS (PROFIT)

A Modern Shaman's Guide to a Pregnant Universe

GODS can be either invisible or visible depending on how well you SEE.

Once humans grow aware of their imitations, they get to learn how to GIVE THANKS to the GODS that work and, most of all, learn how to FIRE the GODS who are no longer getting the jobs done.

DON'T BE FOOLED BY THE AXIOM
"The Greater Thy Trial, the Greater Thy Triumph"
This is popular religious propaganda.

Some believe that CONSCIOUSNESS has been torn from its ROOTS and needs the authority of the GODS in order to survive. MANY believe that the only way that MAN & THE EARTH can survive is if He remains a linked slave to the TUNES OF THE GODS. Some even believe that SORROW & SUFFERING are inevitable and that human nature is solely dependent on the whims of GODS that cannot be FIRED and/or REPLACED.

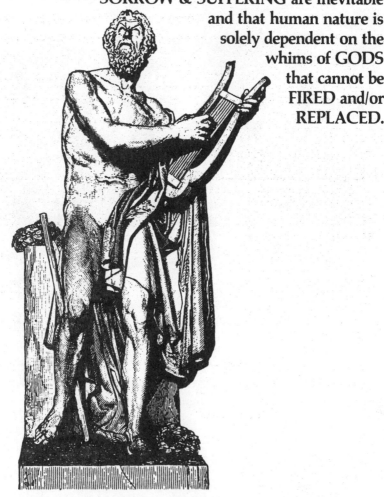

A Modern Shaman's Guide to a Pregnant Universe

ARISE & SHINE
FOR THE LIGHT
HAS COME!

GOD SEPARATION NOTICE

DATE			
ID PROGRAM			

PROGRAM NUMBER	INSECURITY LEVEL	BRAIN LOCALE	EFFECTIVE DATE
		FREE-FALL CLASSIFICATION	HOPE NUMBER

REASON	COMMENTS
☐ DISFUNCTIONAL	
☐ BOREDOM	
☐ RELATIONSHIPS	
☐ FEARS	
☐ TAKING CHANCES	
☐ EXPERIMENTAL JOB	Not eligible for Disability or
☐ QUIT—ELIGIBLE FOR	Unemployment Insurance
RE-EMPLOYMENT: YES ☐ / NO ☐	
☐ OTHER _____	
_____	

	PROGRAM SUPERVISOR	DATE	PERSONNEL DEPARTMENT	DATE
THIS FORM MUST BE COMPLETED AND FILED WITH OFFICE IMMEDIATELY UPON RELEASE OF GODS	META SUPERVISOR	DATE	PAYROLL DEPARTMENT	DATE

On: HIRING A GOD FORM

THE GOD FORM
APPLICATION FOR EMPLOYMENT

NAME: _____   SOCIAL SECURITY # (REQUIRED): _____

ALIASES (use additional pages if necessary): _____
_____

WHAT ARE YOUR QUALIFICATIONS? _____
_____

PERSONAL/PROFESSIONAL REFERENCES: _____
_____

WHAT DO YOU HAVE TO OFFER ME? _____
_____

WHAT PAYMENT DO YOU REQUIRE? _____
_____

HOW MUCH VACATION TIME DO YOU REQUIRE? _____
_____

WHAT GODS/GODDESSES DO YOU GET ALONG WITH? _____
_____

WHAT EXPERIENCES HAVE YOU HAD WITH A PERSON LIKE ME? _____
_____

WHAT ARE YOUR PAST ACCOMPLISHMENTS? _____
_____

HOW WOULD YOU DESCRIBE YOURSELF? _____
_____

HAVE YOU EVER BEEN CONVICTED OF A FELONY? YES ☐   NO ☐

HAVE YOU EVER USED DRUGS? YES ☐   NO ☐

WOULD YOU TAKE A URINE TEST? YES ☐   NO ☐

SINGLE ☐ MARRIED ☐ DIVORCED ☐ SEPARATED ☐ COHABITING ☐

NUMBER OF CHILDREN & THEIR AGES _____
_____

CLOSEST LIVING RELATIVE _____

(THE FOLLOWING IS A SAMPLE APPLICATION FILLED OUT BY POPE NICHOLAS THE ONE ON BEHALF OF JESUS OF NAZARETH)
THE GOD FORM
APPLICATION FOR EMPLOYMENT

NAME: Jesus of Nazareth   **SOCIAL SECURITY # (REQUIRED):** 156-666-9393

ALIASES: (use additional pages if necessary): The Son of God, Christ, Rabbi Jehesua, The Messiah, The Lamb, The Pigeon, *et. al.*

WHAT ARE YOUR QUALIFICATIONS? i am very good at telling stories to childlike peasants and uneducated slaves. i also do a passable magic act.

PERSONAL/PROFESSIONAL REFERENCES: Dozens of Popes, Jimmy Swaggart, Jerry Falwell, Torquemada

WHAT DO YOU HAVE TO OFFER ME? Freedom

WHAT PAYMENT DO YOU REQUIRE? Absolute obedience

HOW MUCH VACATION TIME DO YOU REQUIRE? There are plenty of mortals ready to speak for me, so i don't hang around much anymore. Why take the risk?

WHAT GODS/GODDESSES DO YOU GET ALONG WITH? My Father and the Spook

WHAT EXPERIENCES HAVE YOU HAD WITH A PERSON LIKE ME? Well, Hyatt, people like you tend to ignore me. Or even sneer at me. And write awful things about me—and my mommy!

WHAT ARE YOUR PAST ACCOMPLISHMENTS? Though i taught that men should go along with the dogma of the group with the most powerful weapons, i was murdered anyway when i talked too much. Since then, i've learned to keep quiet and mostly hung around in the background. My lieutenants have done a remarkable job of recruiting more troops and, getting rid of any dissenting humans as well as competing gods and goddesses. So, in numerical terms, i've been one of the most successful gods ever.

HOW WOULD YOU DESCRIBE YOURSELF? i came to be on this strange planet in a manner still a mystery to me. With some success, i was indoctrinated into the monotheistic Judaic culture. i spent a number of years wandering about, learning. Then i tried to communicate what i learned, that there is more to life than the peasant existence and slave mentality most people lived at that time and still do today. At that level i guess i've done a lousy job. Still, i have a great compactness of energy. By teaching in vague parables and leaving most things unspoken, i have enabled humans to interpret me in any way they want. This has allowed me to accumulate maximum power with minimum effort.

HAVE YOU EVER BEEN CONVICTED OF A FELONY? EXPLAIN Yes, for having a big mouth and not having the weapons to back it up.

HAVE YOU EVER USED DRUGS? Yes, but don't tell anyone

WOULD YOU TAKE A URINE TEST? Sure

SINGLE ☐ MARRIED ☑ DIVORCED ☐ SEPARATED ☐ COHABITING ☐

NAME OF SPOUSE: Mary Magdalene, thousands of nuns, priests and monks

DO YOU HAVE AIDS? Well, you know how those priests are

NUMBER OF CHILDREN: i've made everyone my child, whether you like it or not.

THE HIRSTORY OF THE HUMAN RACES
is:
The FEAR & TREMBLING of LIFE ITSELF

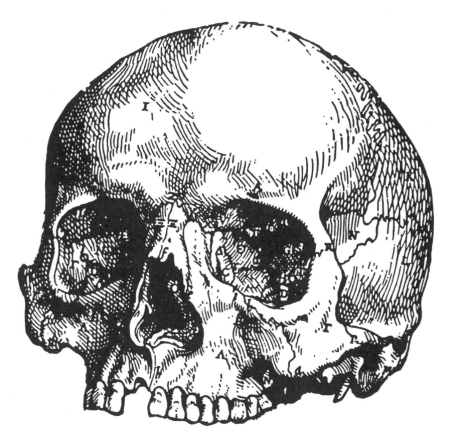

This is best symbolized by the thickness of skin on the knees that has allowed humans to endlessly worship that which promises to remove the HOLY TERRORS.

The MODERN SHAMAN still feels TERROR.
The only difference being that SHe does not require scraping Hir knees. If SHe must get down on Hir knees, SHe is smart enough to wear kneepads.

OR

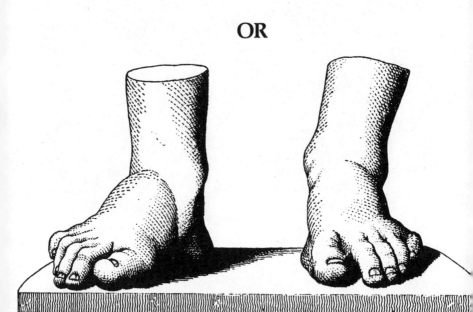

"Learn to Stand On Your Toes"
says Dr. Tim

---

100   *A Modern Shaman's Guide to a Pregnant Universe*

There are
many LEGENDS CIRCULATING that
in order to function at a HIGHER
PSYCHO-NEURAL level, Man must rid
Himself of his EGO.
This is a primal slave dictum.

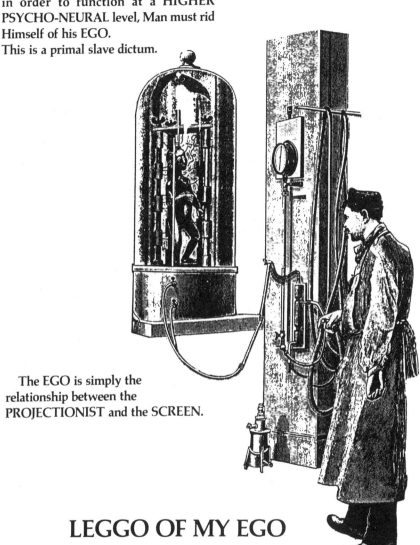

The EGO is simply the
relationship between the
PROJECTIONIST and the SCREEN.

LEGGO OF MY EGO

**What's
a CYBER-
SHAMAN
to do?**

R.S.V.P.

The CYBER-SHAMAN creates his own TEMPLE. He brings his own lights and incense. He purges and purifies himself of not instinct and ego but of IGNORANCE. There are NO collection plates inside a CYBER-TEMPLE. The GODS arrive by: Invitation Only . . .
RSVP.

PHASE 5

BUILDING WORD PRISONS DISMANTLING THEM

WIN — PLACE — SHOW
The Race is One by a Head.

NO PROFESSIONAL VICTIMS
ALLOWED

Welcome to the Word Pharmacy
"Learning to Use Her Head"

PAINTING BIO-CHEMICAL
WORD PICTURES

FINDING YOUR WAY THROUGH THE UNIVERSE

To find your direction for any choice, use the list of BI-POLAR ADJECTIVES to describe your images, thoughts and feelings prior to performing any act (for more info, refer to: *Pharmaceutical Astrology, Phase 3*).

POSITIVE ————————	NEGATIVE
MASCULINE ————————	FEMININE
RADIANT ————————	MAGNETIC
DRY ————————	MOIST
STRONG ————————	WEAK
COLD ————————	HOT
IMPORTANT ————————	INSIGNIFICANT
DOMINANT ————————	SUBMISSIVE
STABLE ————————	VOLATILE
MECHANICAL ————————	SPONTANEOUS
GOOD ————————	EVIL
PLEASURE ————————	PAIN
YOUNG ————————	OLD
COMMITTED ————————	INDIFFERENT
BEAUTIFUL ————————	UGLY
REASON ————————	INTUITION
HARD ————————	SOFT
JOY ————————	SORROW
CREATIVE ————————	DESTRUCTIVE
ILLUSION ————————	REALITY
CLEAR ————————	DENSE
OPEN ————————	CLOSED
SURPRISE ————————	PLAN
FREEDOM ————————	SLAVERY
CERTAIN ————————	UNCERTAIN

When you're done with your performance, re-take the
WORD-DRUGS above and compare your results.

As you become more familiar with the pharmacy, instead of responding to all the chemicals, choose the ones **A/HEAD** of time which might be the most useful.

For example, Hyatt is:

POSITIVE ————————	NEGATIVE
MASCULINE ————————	FEMININE
RADIANT ————————	MAGNETIC
DRY ————————	MOIST
STRONG ————————	WEAK
COLD ————————	HOT
IMPORTANT ————————	INSIGNIFICANT
DOMINANT ————————	SUBMISSIVE
STABLE ————————	VOLATILE
MECHANICAL ————————	SPONTANEOUS
GOOD ————————	EVIL
PLEASURE ————————	PAIN
YOUNG ————————	OLD
COMMITTED ————————	INDIFFERENT
BEAUTIFUL ————————	UGLY
REASON ————————	INTUITION
HARD ————————	SOFT
JOY ————————	SORROW
CREATIVE ————————	DESTRUCTIVE
ILLUSION ————————	REALITY
CLEAR ————————	DENSE
OPEN ————————	CLOSED
SURPRISE ————————	PLAN
FREEDOM ————————	SLAVERY
CERTAIN ————————	UNCERTAIN

NOW TRY ANTERO

POSITIVE — — — — — — — NEGATIVE
MASCULINE — — — — — — — FEMININE
RADIANT — — — — — — — MAGNETIC
DRY — — — — — — — MOIST
STRONG — — — — — — — WEAK
COLD — — — — — — — HOT
IMPORTANT — — — — — — — INSIGNIFICANT
DOMINANT — — — — — — — SUBMISSIVE
STABLE — — — — — — — VOLATILE
MECHANICAL — — — — — — — SPONTANEOUS
GOOD — — — — — — — EVIL
PLEASURE — — — — — — — PAIN
YOUNG — — — — — — — OLD
COMMITTED — — — — — — — INDIFFERENT
BEAUTIFUL — — — — — — — UGLY
REASON — — — — — — — INTUITION
HARD — — — — — — — SOFT
JOY — — — — — — — SORROW
CREATIVE — — — — — — — DESTRUCTIVE
ILLUSION — — — — — — — REALITY
CLEAR — — — — — — — DENSE
OPEN — — — — — — — CLOSED
SURPRISE — — — — — — — PLAN
FREEDOM — — — — — — — SLAVERY
CERTAIN — — — — — — — UNCERTAIN

A Modern Shaman's Guide to a Pregnant Universe

NOW TRY YOURSELF

POSITIVE — — — — — — —	NEGATIVE
MASCULINE — — — — — — —	FEMININE
RADIANT — — — — — — —	MAGNETIC
DRY — — — — — — —	MOIST
STRONG — — — — — — —	WEAK
COLD — — — — — — —	HOT
IMPORTANT — — — — — — —	INSIGNIFICANT
DOMINANT — — — — — — —	SUBMISSIVE
STABLE — — — — — — —	VOLATILE
MECHANICAL — — — — — — —	SPONTANEOUS
GOOD — — — — — — —	EVIL
PLEASURE — — — — — — —	PAIN
YOUNG — — — — — — —	OLD
COMMITTED — — — — — — —	INDIFFERENT
BEAUTIFUL — — — — — — —	UGLY
REASON — — — — — — —	INTUITION
HARD — — — — — — —	SOFT
JOY — — — — — — —	SORROW
CREATIVE — — — — — — —	DESTRUCTIVE
ILLUSION — — — — — — —	REALITY
CLEAR — — — — — — —	DENSE
OPEN — — — — — — —	CLOSED
SURPRISE — — — — — — —	PLAN
FREEDOM — — — — — — —	SLAVERY
CERTAIN — — — — — — —	UNCERTAIN

How are you alike and different from Antero and Hyatt?

Use different color dots or symbols to reference each evaluation then, connect the dots to arrive at your pharmaceutical bio-map.

POSITIVE — — — — — — — NEGATIVE
MASCULINE — — — — — — — FEMININE
RADIANT — — — — — — — MAGNETIC
DRY — — — — — — — MOIST
STRONG — — — — — — — WEAK
COLD — — — — — — — HOT
IMPORTANT — — — — — — — INSIGNIFICANT
DOMINANT — — — — — — — SUBMISSIVE
STABLE — — — — — — — VOLATILE
MECHANICAL — — — — — — — SPONTANEOUS
GOOD — — — — — — — EVIL
PLEASURE — — — — — — — PAIN
YOUNG — — — — — — — OLD
COMMITTED — — — — — — — INDIFFERENT
BEAUTIFUL — — — — — — — UGLY
REASON — — — — — — — INTUITION
HARD — — — — — — — SOFT
JOY — — — — — — — SORROW
CREATIVE — — — — — — — DESTRUCTIVE
ILLUSION — — — — — — — REALITY
CLEAR — — — — — — — DENSE
OPEN — — — — — — — CLOSED
SURPRISE — — — — — — — PLAN
FREEDOM — — — — — — — SLAVERY
CERTAIN — — — — — — — UNCERTAIN

Reproduce for Future Use.

POSITIVE — — — — — — — NEGATIVE
MASCULINE — — — — — — FEMININE
RADIANT — — — — — — — MAGNETIC
DRY — — — — — — — MOIST
STRONG — — — — — — — WEAK
COLD — — — — — — — HOT
IMPORTANT — — — — — — — INSIGNIFICANT
DOMINANT — — — — — — SUBMISSIVE
STABLE — — — — — — — VOLATILE
MECHANICAL — — — — — — — SPONTANEOUS
GOOD — — — — — — — EVIL
PLEASURE — — — — — — — PAIN
YOUNG — — — — — — — OLD
COMMITTED — — — — — — — INDIFFERENT
BEAUTIFUL — — — — — — — UGLY
REASON — — — — — — — INTUITION
HARD — — — — — — — SOFT
JOY — — — — — — — SORROW
CREATIVE — — — — — — — DESTRUCTIVE
ILLUSION — — — — — — — REALITY
CLEAR — — — — — — — DENSE
OPEN — — — — — — — CLOSED
SURPRISE — — — — — — — PLAN
FREEDOM — — — — — — — SLAVERY
CERTAIN — — — — — — — UNCERTAIN

Don't Abuse the Authors

THIS IS

PHASE

6.66

INFORMATION WARS

Historically, humans have fought wars using spears, guns, boats & planes, missiles, and finally . . . atomic bombs to control and destroy each other.

WAR is almost always fought over TERRITORY

As each culture develops and expands, its boundaries start to creep and stretch outward to feed on more TERRITORY to keep growing. As AWEFULL as it is, WAR is a way to LEGALIZE the expansion of territory.

Countless humans have spent and continue to spend their LIFETIMES dedicated to GETTING RID OF WAR by making up LAWS to STOP WAR.

Yet, WAR keeps coming back in larger doses
and packing greater punches than ever.

Some believe that WAR,
like NATURE,
knows no LAWS . . . only NECESSITIES.

IS WAR
NECESSARY
AT THIS TIME?

(How can an entire planet
convert over to Christianity
without war?)

Here now in the INFORMATION AGE we are fighting INFO WARS with PROPAGANDA BOMBS and MIS-INFORMATION MISSILES to control and destroy each others MINDS. As AWEFULL as this is, we now know that the HUMAN MIND is the NEW TURF.

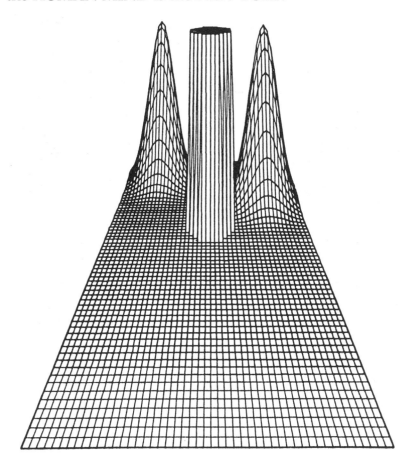

THE CYBER-SHAMAN IS AN INFO-WARRIOR OUT OF NECESSITY

SHe is out on the FRONT LINES using the NEWEST INFO-STRATEGIES to gather data for protecting Hir HARD-EARNED AUTONOMY.

INFO-WARRIORS KNOW HOW TO COVER THEIR ASSETS.

CYBER-SHAMANS ARE PILOTS
navigating their futures NOW amidst the turbulence
of the INFORMATION WARS.

A BOMB SHELL-TER BY DR. TIM
(*Info Psychology:* Falcon Press 1987)

Period	Stage of Evolution
1. Bio-Survival (Marine) Stages	1. Invertebrate 2. Marine-vertebrate 3. Amphibian
2. The Terrestrial Mammalian Stages	4. Evasive Mammalian 5. Predator Mammalian 6. Hunter-Gatherer
3. The Symbolic Tool Stage	7. Tool User, Paleolithic 8. Tool Maker, Neolithic 9. Tribal, Metal Age
4. Industrial	10. Feudal 11. National, Low Industrial 12. Multi-National, High Industrial
5. Cyber-Somatic Piloting Sensory Info	13. Individual Consumer Hedonism 14. Individual Aesthetic Mastery 15. Hedonic-Aesthetic Linkage
6. Cyber-Electronic Piloting Quantum Electronic Info	16. Individual Consumer Access to Brain and Electronic Technology 17. Individual Mastering of Brain and Electronic Technology 18. Neuro-Electronic Networks
7. Cyber-Genetic Piloting DNA/RNA Data	19. Individual Brain Management through Genetic Technology 20. Individual Mastery of Genetic Technology Information 21. Electronic Networks - Linkage of Genetic Technology Information
8. Cyber-Nano-Tech Piloting Atomic Info	22. Individual Consumer Access to Nano-Tech (Atomic Information) 23. Individual Mastery of Nano-Tech (Atomic Information) 24. Nano Technological Linkage

Every Shaman has ways to protect the
HOT, NEW SACRED TURF
of their Freedom.

CYBER-SHAMANS
call upon the allegiance of "SPIRIT ALLIES"
(see *Pharmaceutical Astrology*)
to shapeshift and change their forms to
CAMOUFLAGE their intentions during WARTIME.

CYBER-ARTILLERY
has been designed NOT to destroy minds but to
DISMANTLE obsolete thinking and thus, set up a
WOMB WITH A VIEW
by impregnating defenseless minds with the
SURPRISING FACTS of NEW INFORMATION.

Remember: **Modern Shamans are MIDWIVES to a PREGNANT UNIVERSE and BABY GODS can only incubate inside the New Information of OMNIDIRECTIONAL CONSCIOUSNESS ...**

**HYATT'S
NUMBER ONE
PROPOSITION
FOR FUTURE
MUTANTS**

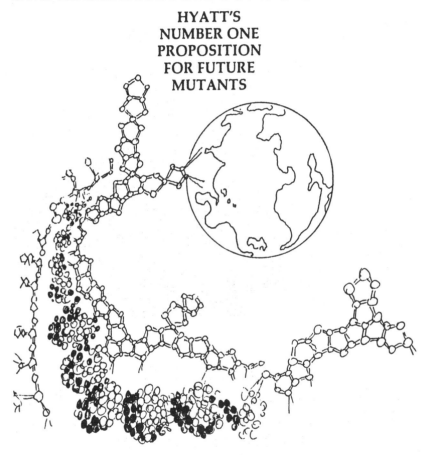

**CULTURE IS THE RESULT OF THE
INTERACTION OF GENETICS & GEOGRAPHY**

NEW INFO INJECTIONS
ARE
NOW AVAILABLE.

DISORDER and DAT ORDER
are polar functions of a larger governing body called
NEW INFORMATION

1) A vortex of DISORDER makes it impossible to predict what will happen next.

2) DAT ORDER is a matrix of useable messages.

Remember: The new definition of information (NEO-INFO) is the unpredictability of a message.

The NEW INFORMATION arrives as soon as you realize how DISORDER and DAT ORDER work together in the JOINT VENTURE of their overlapping vortrex/matrix vectors. Also known as HEMI-SYNC, the synchronization of left and right hemispheres of the BRAINS.

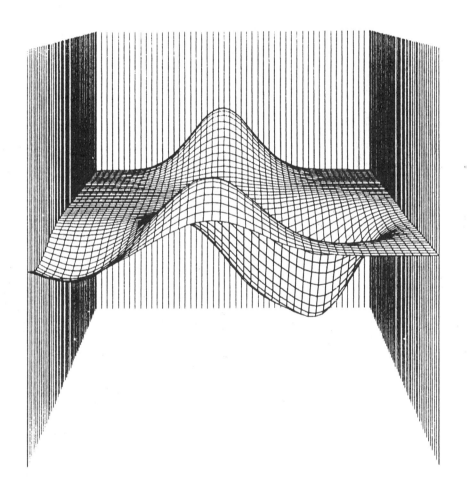

The
most devastating,
sophisticated
form of
INFO-WARFARE
is:
**TELLING
THE
TRUTH**

(not to be confused with SELLING THE TRUTH)

Due to the unspoken law prohibiting TELLING THE TRUTH in Public Places, the CYBER-SHAMAN resorts to camouflage-tactics like HUMOR, MYTHOLOGY, POETRY, MUSIC, ENTERTAINMENT and other IMPROVISATIONAL TURN-ONS ... to score a direct hit. (Everybody loves a GOOD SHOW.)

Get around the Gargoyles of the Threshold (culturally conditioned mind-censors) and you're in.

P.S. The Gargoyles of the Threshold are also known as the Terrible Council of the Hideous Corpuscle.

BEARING UP
"A Bedtime Nightmare Story"

One day a long time ago a very intelligent and compassionate man told me that there were only a few things in life which he couldn't bear.

I asked him what he meant by that. He responded "something which he felt he couldn't live with, something which he couldn't stand up under."

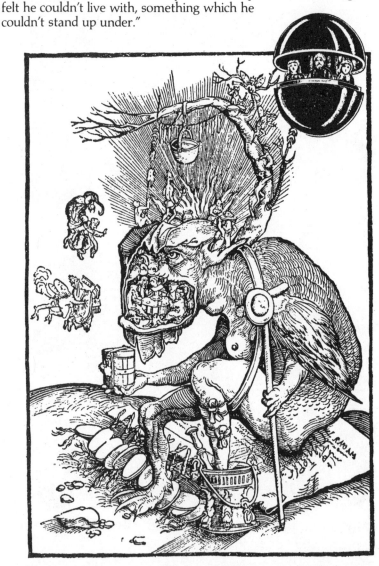

I got a feeling for what he was saying. He was talking about the UNBEARABLE

A Modern Shaman's Guide to a Pregnant Universe

For most of us
the UNBEARABLE is buried
away deep in our minds.
It is beyond shame
and humiliation, although
components of these may be
present. It often includes the
possibility of BEING
OUT OF CONTROL

WARNING!
ENTITY
OUT
OF
CONTROL!

I began conceptualizing the UNBEARABLE as a corpuscle buried somewhere deep in the psyche with almost invisible tentacles reaching out to affect our entire life.

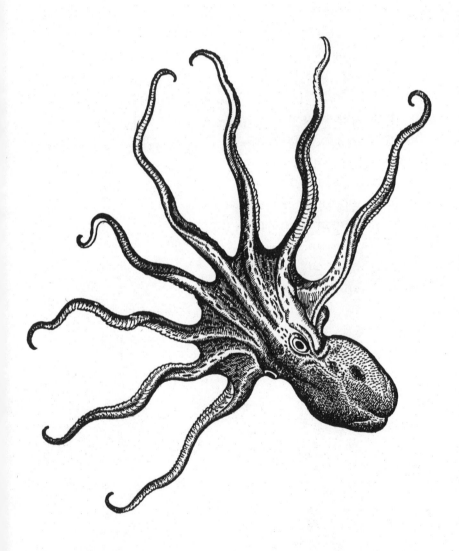

A Modern Shaman's Guide to a Pregnant Universe

With this nightmare in mind, I ventured out and gathered information which supported my thesis. About 96% of the people I spoke with were able to admit, recall, or identify some event or thing which they thought was unbearable. However, only 59% admitted to having any daily, weekly, or monthly awareness of the UNBEARABLE. Fewer yet, about 24% were aware that the UNBEARABLE was affecting how they functioned NOW.

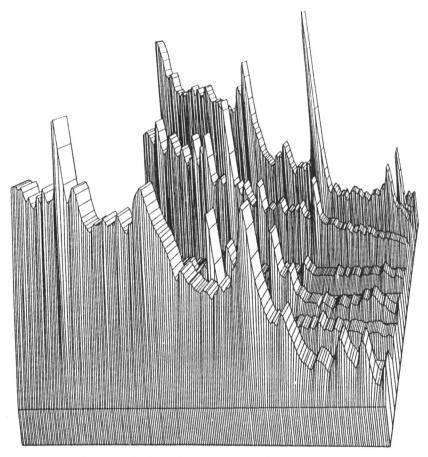

About 6% agreed that their FEAR of the UNBEARABLE restricted their progress in life and the manifestation of their "true will," or life "calling."

One Individual likened it to EXTREME STAGE FRIGHT, where she was lost for words, and the entire audience laughed and pointed at her. She even imagined that she lost bladder control and urinated all over herself. In the telling of her story we could sense her physiological terror.

A Modern Shaman's Guide to a Pregnant Universe

Another Individual had an image of his son killing himself. He thought that if this ever happened he could no

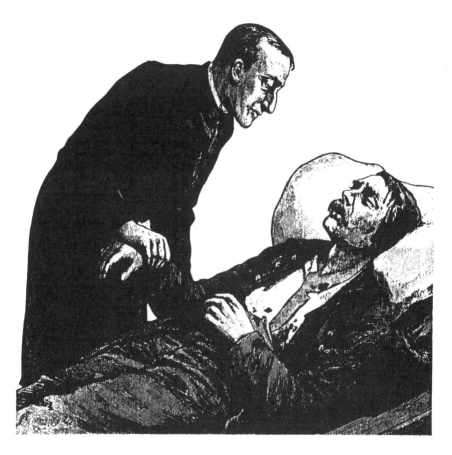

longer live with himself. His life would end. Everything he stood for would disappear.

Still another Individual who couldn't identify an Unbearable phantasy in the here and now, likened it to being a ten year old boy in a shower with adult men. All the adult males were laughing at his small penis.

Regardless

of what the UnBearable was for each person, each seemed entranced, wide-eyed, almost fixed in terror.

A Modern Shaman's Guide to a Pregnant Universe

The moment passed, and we both retreated to normal consciousness.

Waking up from nightmares which we are aware of is a relief. However, living in nightmares of which we have little or no awareness, unable to wake up from is no doubt an awesome fact, something which, if we could all awaken from would put an end to the slavery-master metaphor which has immobilized our greatest planetary resource—THE BRAINS.

CHILDREN HAVE NIGHTMARES IN ORDER TO WAKE UP.

A Modern Shaman's Guide to a Pregnant Universe

The POWER of the UNBEARABLE is to restrict the free flow form of the individual. It is as if it acts as a prison, made of images, words and expectations. Vast human potential is lost AND DISSIPATED AS HEAT to a greedy atmosphere.

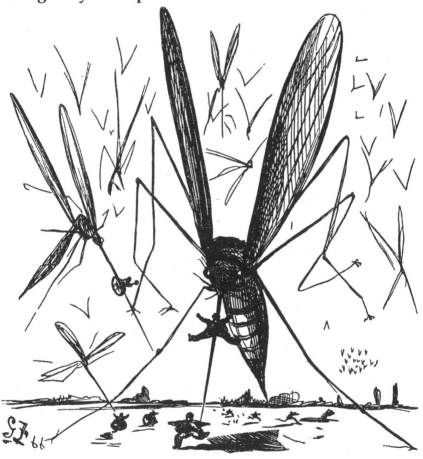

The awesome Power of the Unbearable RESTRICTS our thoughts, feelings, actions, bodies and lifestyles flows.

WE COMMAND YOU!
OR ... IF YOU CHOOSE DO IT ...
IT IS EASY AS 1 ... 2 ... 3 ... ?????

1. Find the corpuscle.
2. Look into its Hideous Hairy Heart.
3. BARE the anxiety of the SHOCK.

A Modern Shaman's Guide to a Pregnant Universe

The Beast is Dead,
the Gods are born.

Contractions pain the doors of the prison,
the womb tears loose and they are
BORN AGAIN.

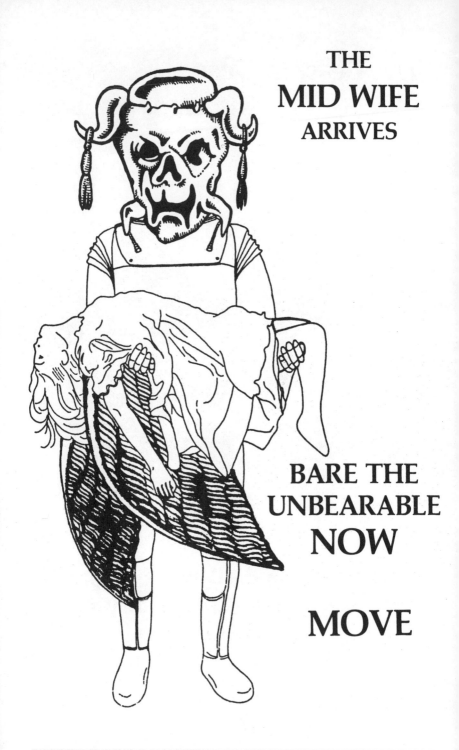

THE
MID WIFE
ARRIVES

BARE THE
UNBEARABLE
NOW

MOVE

People have been known to live in the same place, do the same thing day in and day out of fear that the Unbearable might happen.

One could say that the CorPusCle of the Unbearable acts like a GOVERNMENT making sure of the whereabouts of its citizens.

CURFEW IS NOW ACTIVE
RETURN TO UNIT

The corpuscle metaphor with octopus tentacles invisibly reaching and extending into the depths of our lives seems to be a workable and ENGAGING notion expressing and reinforcing the idea that words and images can and do act as drugs expanding and limiting our lives.

The TERRIBLE COUNCIL of
the HIDEOUS CORPUSCLE is
is
is SUMMONING YOU (YOUR) NOW.

Becoming aware of and identifying your
SECRET NIGHTMARES
and not-so secret

CAT/TASK/TROPHIES
AND your very own personal UNBEARABLES. This
NEW INFO contains one of the remaining primal
secrets which can actually free you and open you up to
the possibilities of a PREGNANT UNIVERSE awaiting
the Mid-Wifery of the CYBER-SHAMAN.

Mr. Crowley said:

"Restriction is Sin." If we need sin, let it be the metaphor of image and word restriction.

— LEGGO NOW —
Hold On to the Metaphor

THE FINAL SECRET OF THE ILLUMINATI

NINO

NOTHING IN NOTHING OUT

PHASE 777

METANOIDS

DON'T BE AFRAID OF A METANOID:
Cyber-Enemas for Cyber Enemies

By standing up for something, you invariably end up turning your back on something else.

BY V'SAR 23

Everybody KNOWS who THE ENEMY is. (Don't you?)
THE ENEMY is anyone who works, either intentionally and/or automatically,

to DESTROY YOU.

We know who the ENEMY is and how to identify the STENCH. CYBER-SHAMANS track the habits of the ENEMY and locate its habitat.

BY V'SAR 23

We know what the ENEMY eats and when it sleeps. CYBER-SHAMANS hunt the ENEMY before they are hunted themselves.

We know the ENEMY IS WITHIN and that it would GLOAT at the chance to DOMINATE & RELINQUISH our True Will.

CYBER-SHAMANS choose SILLY ENEMIES.
We know how important it is to LAUGH AT DEATH.

BY V'SAR 23

A Modern Shaman's Guide to a Pregnant Universe

One particularly SILLY ENEMY of the CYBER-SHAMAN is
THE METANOID.

METANOIDS are Inactive Philosophers immobilized by their insight.
METANOIDS read more than they write, work more than they play,
and always understand much more than they KNOW. METANOIDS
are especially fond of understanding complex metaphysical treatises
without having tested anything in THE LAB of REAL LIFE.
METANOIDS are MEGA-NERDS.

This is why they are SILLY yet DANGEROUS, HARMLESS yet FATAL,
OFTEN FRIENDLY & SINCERE yet . . . the INSIPID ENEMY,itself.

The CYBER-SHAMAN is astonished by the profound
MODESTY of its ENEMY, the METANOID who
would never dream of actually
BEING A MID-WIFE,
TAKING ON GOD FORMS,
OWNING A PHARMACY
SURVIVING THE INFORMATION WARS,
or ENTERING THE HIDEOUS CORPUSCLE . . .

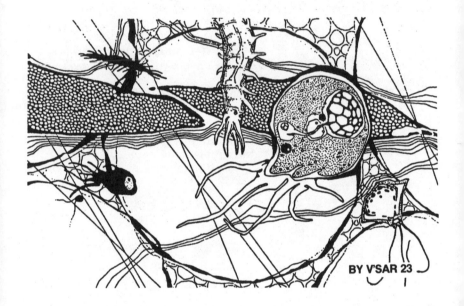

for Fear of Imposing.

INTENTIONAL SUFFERING FOR FUN AND PROFIT

On the planet Earth suffering is essential.
On planet Earth humans suffer as a simple consequence of gravity.
On Planet Earth Humans suffer as a simple consequence of being Human.

There is no way out of suffering.

But there is a way into knowing
that suffering is frequently
impersonal and:

that by personalizing suffering,
in a non-paranoid way, that is,
you can develop a "soul"
a real "I's."

A Modern Shaman's Guide to a Pregnant Universe

Do not mis-understand,
suffering is neither moral nor immoral.

These are simply "necessary" categories for the human mind.
They help it to believe in "justice" and "order," both
"essential" placebofors for apparent smooth functioning.

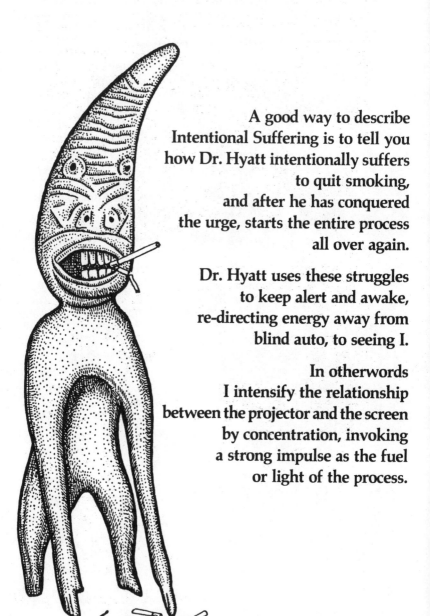

A good way to describe
Intentional Suffering is to tell you
how Dr. Hyatt intentionally suffers
to quit smoking,
and after he has conquered
the urge, starts the entire process
all over again.

Dr. Hyatt uses these struggles
to keep alert and awake,
re-directing energy away from
blind auto, to seeing I.

In otherwords
I intensify the relationship
between the projector and the screen
by concentration, invoking
a strong impulse as the fuel
or light of the process.

Intentional Suffering is a frantic yoga of the brain.

However, place no moral value on what I do,
or what you might decide to do yourself.

Remember **INTENTION is what makes an accident a CRIME.**

GLOSSARY
by
Dr. Tim

EXO-PSYCHOLOGY: The psychology of post-terrestrial existence.

INFO-PSYCHOLOGY: The psychology of the post-industrial society. Precedes and complements Exo-Psychology.

DIGITAL LANGUAGE OR QUANTUM LINGUISTICS: Thoughts packaged, stored, processed and communicated in terms of quantitative patterns. H_2O is the digitized (quantum) expression for lettered thoughts such as "wasser," "l'eau," "agua," "water."

SPACE: The extra-terrestrial universe, the solar system, stars, galaxies usually defined as material structures.

INFO-SPACE: Our world, the galaxy, the universe defined and measured in terms of information. The quantum universe of signals, bits, digital elements, recorded by, stored in, processed, communicated by electronic knowledge technology, the human brain and its electronic extensions.

LARYNGEAL-MANUAL (L-M): Oral, hand-crafted language. The creation of hand-made artifacts and tools. The paleolithic, neolithic and tool-making (tribal) stages of human evolution which came after hunter-gatherer and before feudal, industrial and quantum stages.

LARVAL: Early primitive stages of human evolution which precede space migration and attainment of individual mastery of quantum technology. LARVAL humans are instinctively, reflexively tied to collectives; they have not reached the cyber (pilot) states of auto-thinking. This term is deliberately insolent and provocative. To label fellow human beings as belonging to primitive stages of evolution does not insure immediate popularity. This satirical usage reflects the author's traditional, Celtic playful arrogance, here inflated by jail-house blues.

DOMESTICATED PRIMATES: Humans who do not think for themselves. Human beings who belong to tribes, states, churches, rigid organizations, nations, industrial societies. The stages which precede individual cyber-life. This is another typical snide Sufi (Gurdjieffian) barb at people who do not think for themselves. An "in joke" not appreciated by some. (Informative and funny references to DP's can be found in the following Falcon Press books presented in the order of snideness, *Undoing Yourself, Prometheus Rising, Angel Tech,* and *Breaking the GodSpell.*)

POST-SYMBOLIC: Stages of thinking which use digitized clusters of quanta rather than lettered words or vocal utterances.

COLLECTIVE: All stages of human evolution which precede individual independence. Other synonyms: member of HIVE, HERD, FLOCK. Usually used with satirical intent (See *Undoing Yourself*).

TERRESTRIAL: Stages which precede space-migration and cyber-quantum thinking.

QUANTUM: The word "quantum" refers to a bit, an elemental unit. The word QUANTUM used as an adjective indicates that the subject is defined in terms of numbers, clusters of digitized elements, units of information.

QUANTUM PHYSICS OR INFO-PHYSICS: This is contrasted with the mechanical, material physics of Newton which concerned itself with such issues as mass, force, work, energy.

QUANTUM PHYSICS: Defines a universe made up of temporary clusters of info-units, elemental off-on, digital bits.

THE QUANTUM UNIVERSE: Is an INFO-UNIVERSE.

QUANTUM PHYSICS REFERS TO INFORMATION SCIENCE: The decoding of the signals of the universe in the many dimensions of complexity. Whereas the Newtonian universe was composed of apparently solid matter, the INFO-UNIVERSE is made up of data structures.

THE QUANTUM PERSON: Inhabits data-space, lives in Info-Worlds.

QUANTUM PSYCHOLOGY: A synonym for EXO-PSYCHOLOGY. Human thought and behavior described in terms of the language of numbers, computers, icons.

THE ROARING 20th CENTURY: Each decade of the 20th Century has witnessed the emergence of information appliances and new communication-art-forms which give human increasing access to and control of electronic (digital) information. The quantum appliances include telephones, radio, phonographs, movies, television, portable cassette players, CB radios, home synthesizers, compact disks.

CYBER: The word CYBER comes from the Greek *kubernetes*, pilot. The Heisenberg principle demonstrated that the observer determines (i.e. defines) the realities SHe confronts by the nature of the observational technologies and the maps/models used for interpretation.

THE CYBER-PERSON: Is the individual who understands the Heisenberg principle and accepts responsibility for the realities SHe defines and inhabits.

This general principle of Self-Determination has been described for millennia by Hindu-Buddhist-Gnostic-Sufi philosophers. Creative people, writers, artists, poets, dramatists, inventors, innovators, shamans, intelligent magicians have, throughout the centuries, understood this principle. They have used it to fabricate the glories of human culture and science. However, the ability of CYBER-PERSONS to create realities has been limited to symbols, icons, myths, scripts, artistic and philosophic expressions. The Information structures we call art. Until recently human ability to describe quantum realities could not extend to the material plane because of techno-quantum ignorance. During the Pre-Industrial humans, from philosophers to sultans to serfs, were helpless victims of techno-myopia. The Industrial era tremendously advanced human ability to manage material reality, on the collective scale. It was only in the Roaring 20th Century that humans discovered that the universe is an Info-Structure to be explored and managed by Intelligence, i.e., Cyber-Quantum proficiency to think and build with clusters of digitized thoughts.

CYBER-QUANTUM PSYCHOLOGY: The individual accesses and pilots electronic knowledge technology for hir own personal purposes. The traditional eight attitudes of philosophy can now be re-defined in terms of CYBER-QUANTUM PSYCHOLOGY.

1. COSMOLOGY: The theory of origins defined in Cyber of Collective terms. QUANTUM COSMOLOGY: A theory of origins which can be expressed in scientific, quantum, numerical form.

2. POLITICS: A theory of domination, control, freedom, submission defined either in terms of Individuals (cyber) or collectives. QUANTUM POLITICS: A theory of domination, control, freedom expressed in psycho-geometric coordinates and digital language. See the computer software program MIND MIRROR.

3. EPISTOMOLOGY: The theory which defines truth (cyber-individual belief) and fact (collective-social belief). QUANTUM EPISTOMOLOGY: Truth and fact expressed in digital language and quantum physical descriptions.

4. ETHICS: The theory which defines good/evil (cyber-subjective) and virtue/vice (social-collective). QUANTUM ETHICS: Good and virtue defined in the astro-physical language of psycho-geometry.

5. AESTHETICS: A theory defining subjective-beauty and social-art, personal pleasure and rewards from the collective. QUANTUM AESTHETICS: Beauty, art, pleasure, reward defined in terms of numbers, digits, geometrics.

6. ONTOLOGY: A theory about the nature of reality based on Cyber (personal) or Collective-social attitude.

QUANTUM ONTOLOGY: A theory about the nature of reality defined in scientific, technological, quantum digitese.

7. TELEOLOGY: A theory of evolution, devolution or stasis based on either Cyber-individual or Collective-social attitudes.
QUANTUM TELEOLOGY: A theory of evolution, devolution, or stasis based on measurable indices, quantitative patterns, geometrics.

8. ESCHATOLOGY: A theory of endings, both cyber-individual and collective-social. A person who is not in charge of hir own endings probably cannot fabricate a general theory of evolutionary endings.
QUANTUM ESCHATOLOGY: A theory of endings based upon quantification, digitization, geometry.

Good-bye for now . . .

Thank you for performing this book with us. It has been a pleasure participating in the project of birthing a new species.

It is safe to say that we are not alone. And yet . . .

See you in THE FUTURE.
Hyatt & Alli
Alli & Hyatt

POSITIVE	NEGATIVE
MASCULINE	FEMININE
RADIANT	MAGNETIC
DRY	MOIST
STRONG	WEAK
COLD	HOT
IMPORTANT	INSIGNIFICANT
DOMINANT	SUBMISSIVE
STABLE	VOLATILE
MECHANICAL	SPONTANEOUS
GOOD	EVIL
PLEASURE	PAIN
YOUNG	OLD
COMMITTED	INDIFFERENT
BEAUTIFUL	UGLY
REASON	INTUITION
HARD	SOFT
JOY	SORROW
CREATIVE	DESTRUCTIVE
ILLUSION	REALITY
CLEAR	DENSE
OPEN	CLOSED
SURPRISE	PLAN
FREEDOM	SLAVERY
CERTAIN	UNCERTAIN

NEW AGE MISCARRIAGE
(Or, When the Lion Lies Down with the Lamb)

The incubation of Baby Gods has Nothing to Do with "The New Age" *(as advertised)*.

THE NEW AGE *(as advertised)* IS:

1) the soft, white underbelly of Christianity

2) the Sister Movement of the Great White Fundamentalist Brotherhood

3) a highly successful yet short-lived marketing commodity

NEW AGE AXIOMS, LIKE:

a. All Is One

b. Peace, Light & Harmony

c. I Create My Own Reality

are suffering Last Gasp, obsolete status in the Real World of Multiplicity, Increasing Chaos and Spineless, Robotic People.

Therefore, the NEW AGE *(as advertised)* is:
COSMIC FOO FOO

The Death of this NEW AGE *(by MisCarriage)*
Occurred shortly after
HARMONIC CONVERGENCE
In the Post-Convergence Dead Zones.
(Were you buried or, did you attend the funeral?)

The Dead Foetus has returned
To the Ground of Collective Being . . .

                                        as Fertilizer
Feeding the Future Births of Baby Gods.

New Agers are the Sacrificial Lambs.
Willing to die for the Baby Gods.
This is how the Lion lies down with the Lamb:
Only after it has been fed.

P.S. The AGE of AQUARIUS is a Mask
      for the Return of LEO . . . King of the Beasts

Dr. Hyatt's
RADICAL UNDOING
The Complete Course
for Undoing Yourself

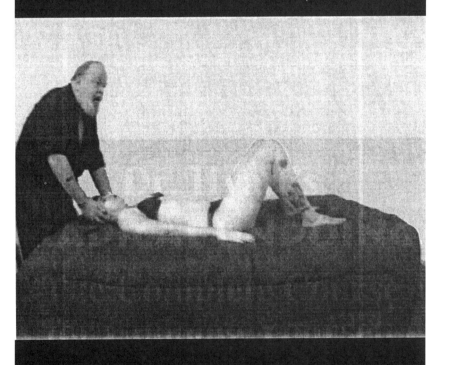

by
Christopher S. Hyatt, Ph.D.

Celebrate Per-Mutation
Goddess Forms Abound
Rebirth to Rebirth to Re- Re- Re-Birth
of a Species

Salutations!

Remember: **A WOMB IS NOT A TOMB IF IT HAS A VISION**

FROM CHRISTOPHER S. HYATT, Ph.D.

SECRETS OF WESTERN TANTRA
The Sexuality of the Middle Path

Introduced by J.M. Spiegelman, Ph.D.
Preface by Robert Anton Wilson

Dr. Hyatt reveals secret methods of enlightenment through transmutation of the *orgastic reflex*. Filled with explicit, practical techniques.

"The world's first scientific experimental yoga that does not expurgate the sensory-sensual-sexual aspects of the Great Work."
—Robert Anton Wilson

ISBN 1-56184-113-7

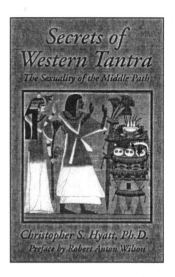

SEX MAGICK, TANTRA & TAROT
The Way of the Secret Lover

With Lon Milo DuQuette
Illustrated by David P. Wilson

A wealth of practical and passionate Tantric techniques utilizing the Archetypal images of the Tarot. Nothing is held back. All methods are explicit and clearly described.

"Each of us has a Guardian Angel — a companion and lover who waits just behind the images that flood our minds during sleep or reverie."

ISBN 1-56184-044-0

FROM CHRISTOPHER S. HYATT, PH.D.

THE PSYCHOPATH'S BIBLE

With Jack Willis & Nicholas Tharcher

Throughout time, psychopaths have gotten a bad rap. That is quite understandable since almost all of the world's religious and social philosophies have little use for the individual except as a tool to be placed in service to their notion of something else: "God," or the "collective," or the "higher good" or some other equally undefinable term. Here, finally, is a book which celebrates, encourages and educates the best part of ourselves — The Psychopath.

ISBN 1-56184-172-2

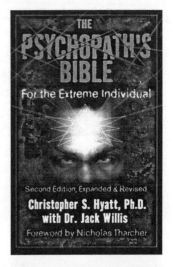

TO LIE IS HUMAN

Not Getting Caught Is Divine

Introduced by Robert Anton Wilson

Take a tour of the prison erected by the lies that society tells you...and the lies you tell yourself. Then, learn the tools to tunnel out...

"Is it possible to use language to undo the hallucinations created by language? ...a few heroic efforts seem able to jolt readers awake... to transcend words."

—Robert Anton Wilson

ISBN 1-56184-199-4

FROM CHRISTOPHER S. HYATT, Ph.D.

UNDOING YOURSELF WITH ENERGIZED MEDITATION

Introduced by Dr. Israel Regardie

Preface by Robert Anton Wilson

A new edition of Dr. Hyatt's incredible, ground-breaking book with 64 pages of brand new material.

"...the Energized Meditation system is fun and erotic and makes you smarter..." Extensively illustrated.

"*Undoing Yourself* is the latest attempt by the Illuminati Conspiracy to reveal the hither-to hidden teachings." — Robert Anton Wilson

ISBN 1-56184-057-2

PACTS WITH THE DEVIL
A Chronicle of Sex, Blasphemy & Liberation

With S. Jason Black

Braving the new Witchcraft Panic that is sweeping America, *Pacts With The Devil* places the Western magical tradition and the Western psyche in perspective. Contains a detailed history of European 'Black Magic' and includes new editions of 17th and 18th century Grimoires with detailed instruction for their use. Extensively illustrated.

ISBN 1-56184-058-0

FROM CHRISTOPHER S. HYATT, Ph.D.

URBAN VOODOO
A Beginner's Guide to Afro-Caribbean Magic

With S. Jason Black

Voodoo, Santeria and Macumba as practiced today in cities throughout the Western world. Includes descriptions of the phenomena triggered by Voodoo practice, divination techniques, spells and a method of self-initiation. Illustrated.

ISBN 1-56184-059-9

ALEISTER CROWLEY'S ILLUSTRATED GOETIA
Sexual Evocation

With Aleister Crowley & Lon Milo DuQuette

Illustrated by David P. Wilson

'*Goetia* [refers to] all the operations of that Magick which deals with gross, malignant or unenlightened forces.' Crowley's *Goetia* is brought to life with vivid illustrations of the demons. Commentary by Crowley experts DuQuette and Hyatt bring the ancient arts into the modern day.

ISBN 1-56184-048-3

FROM CHRISTOPHER S. HYATT, PH.D.

TANTRA WITHOUT TEARS

With S. Jason Black

For the Westerner, this is the only book on Tantra you will ever need. A bold statement? Perhaps. However, the idea behind this book is simple. It is power. It is Kundalini, dressed in Western clothes. It describes experiences and techniques which allow you to glimpse beyond ordinary day-to-day reality, into the world of marvels — and horrors — of the Hindu and Tibetan Tantric traditions.

ISBN 1-56184-060-2

REBELS & DEVILS
The Psychology of Liberation

Contributions by Wm. S. Burroughs, Timothy Leary, Robert Anton Wilson, Aleister Crowley, A.O. Spare, Jack Parsons, Genesis P-Orridge, and many, many others.

"When he put the gun to my head at 16 I left home…" So begins this remarkable book which brings together some of the most talented, controversial and rebellious people *ever.* Not to be missed!

ISBN 1-56184-121-8

FROM CHRISTOPHER S. HYATT, Ph.D.

TABOO

Sex, Religion & Magic

With Lon DuQuette & Gary Ford

Introduced by Robert Anton Wilson

The extensive case histories and rituals expose the *unspeakable taboo* of the West: the union of sex and religion.

"I think it is safe to say that every organized group of idiots will regard this book as extremely dangerous."
　　　　　　　　—Robert Anton Wilson

ISBN 1-56184-039-4

THE ENOCHIAN WORLD OF ALEISTER CROWLEY

Enochian Sex Magick

With Aleister Crowley & Lon Milo DuQuette

Many consider Enochiana the most powerful and least understood system of Western Occult practice. For the first time this esoteric subject is made truly accessible and easy to understand. Includes an Enochian dictionary, extensive illustrations and detailed instructions for the integration of Enochiana with Sex Magick.

ISBN 1-56184-029-7

FROM CHRISTOPHER S. HYATT, PH.D.

TECHNIQUES FOR UNDOING YOURSELF (2 CDs)

With S. Jason Black, Zehm Aloim and Israel Regardie

Dr. Hyatt presents effective methods to change your self and your life! A great companion to Hyatt's ground-breaking book, *Undoing Yourself With Energized Meditation and Other Devices;* adds an entirely new dimension to your repertoire of powerful and dynamic methods of self-change.

ISBN 1-56184-280-X

THE MAGIC OF ISRAEL REGARDIE (2 CDs)

With Zehm Aloim

A frank, in-depth discussion of the many facets and beliefs of one of the world's great mystical adepts, Israel Regardie. Regardie, the author of *The Complete Golden Dawn System of Magic* and many other works, is rightfully considered the greatest proponent of the Golden Dawn. Christopher Hyatt lived and worked with Regardie and knew him better than anyone alive today.

ISBN 1-56184-230-3

New Falcon Publications

Invites You to Visit Our Website:
http://www.newfalcon.com

At the Falcon website you can:

- Browse the online catalog of all of our great titles
- Find out what's available and what's out of stock
- Get special discounts
- Order our titles through our secure online server
- Find products not available anywhere else including:
    - One of a kind and limited availability products
    - Special packages
    - Special pricing
- Get free gifts
- Join our email list for advance notice of New Releases and Special Offers
- Find out about book signings and author events
- Send email to our authors (including the elusive Dr. Christopher Hyatt!)
- Read excerpts of many of our titles
- Find links to our author's websites
- Discover links to other weird and wonderful sites
- And much, much more

Get online today at http://www.newfalcon.com